HEALING ME FOR ME

IWOSON MI FUN MI

**ORISABIYI OYIN
WILLIAMS**

FOREWORD BY

CHIEF EGUNWALE FAGBENRO AMUSAN

EDITED BY

MICHELLE ATKINS

TABLE OF CONTENTS

DEDICATION

I dedicate this book to my children. I love you two to life and beyond.

Whitney Williams (Adebisi)

Billie Foster III (Ekundayo)

ACKNOWLEDGMENTS

Gratitude opens the door to the power, the wisdom and the creativity of the Universe.
–Deepak

First and foremost, I give the deepest thanks to God and my Ancestors. Thank you for guiding me through my journey and making this possible for me.

Thanks to my father, Willie A Williams for always making sure I always had the best of everything and teaching me to be a leader. I have always admired your strength and courage, and you will always be my first love.

Thanks to my mother, Mary Morgan Williams-Anthony. I am forever grateful to you for always being there for me and helping me through the good and the bad. You truly define resilience and courage.

Thanks to my children Whitney and Billie for working with me through those long days of me juggle community work with family. You have inspired me through the ups and downs that we've experienced. I am truly proud that you chose me to be your mom.

Thank you to my sister Kimberly Williams and to Amir Jackson for all the support. Thank you to Kapture Photography for providing the photographs and designs.

Iba se to my brother Kenny A Williams. Thank you for always watching over me on this earth and from a far. You taught me how to take up for myself, and I will never forget the love you have always shown me.

Iba se to my Aunt Ann (Dorothy Vaughn). Your spirit continues to be with me today. Thank you for always encouraging my creativity.

Iba se to my friend Lee Roy Chapman. Thank you for inspiring me and teaching me so much! I miss you!

Big thanks to my family for supporting everything I have done, and never questioning me but motivating me. Thank you for being there for my children and teaching me that family is all we have.

Quinton Morgan, thank you for inspiring me to even write this book. If not for you, I never would have written this book. I can't thank you enough for helping me through this process and calling to ask me; "How much did you write today?" I am forever grateful to you for sharing your success and knowledge with me.

Thank you Chief Egunwale Amusan for teaching me how to die and become the person I am, and continue to become. You truly were that light at the end of the tunnel for me. Everything in this book came from your teachings. I'm grateful you shared your light with me. You are the best Babalowa there is.

Thanks to all my friends from real life to social media and beyond. All of you have left impressions on my life through dialogues, arguments and good times.

FOREWORD

Have you ever wished you could watch the gentle stages of a flower grow from seed to fully bloomed? Orisabiyi Williams has truly given me that pleasure. I have especially had the pleasure of watching her die only to give birth to a better version of herself. This book is an honest look into the life, and transformation of someone just like you. Someone searching for identity, purpose and most importantly love. This book is written from a level of awareness that is in a constant state of change, therefore making this writing very organic in nature. Over the years I have witnessed this outspoken, fierce activist, mother of two go through some extraordinary changes spiritually, emotionally, and physically. This book is the manifestation of many teachings that have helped Africans and other indigenous people throughout the diaspora maintain a sense of humanity, and spiritual wellbeing. In the summer of 2015 I officiated over the naming ceremony of Kristi Williams who is now known as

Orisabiyi. Her name means born of the Orisa(forces of nature). Her destiny revealed that she was born to be a great motivator. I am certain that during that time she had not imagined that she would be writing a book a few months later. Destiny has proven to be a remarkable thing. Ancestral wisdom presents itself as you journey into the pages of this book.

You will be entertained, overwhelmed with curiosity, and immensely encouraged by stories that will inspire you, and in some ways be a reflection of you. The path that Orisabiyi has followed is her own unique path. I am certain that it will become a stepping stone to help you improve, or possibly find your own path. This book takes a holistic approach at looking critically into this thing we call the human experience that in all actuality is uniquely spiritual. Within each chapter of this book there is a seed being planted, and you are the benefactor of its fruits. May this work illuminate your mind, and heal your soul.

Ase!

Chief Egunwale Fagbenro Amusan

INTRODUCTION

At the age of 35 I took a look at myself and didn't like who I was or where I was going. In this book I share some of my experiences and the friendship I have with my cousin Chief. That friendship took me on a journey that forever changed me and continues to change me each day. I wanted to write a book that was an easy read and give you tools on how to deal with everyday life. You will read about how powerful your thoughts, intentions, sex, Black Wall Street, North Tulsa, and why it is important to understand who you are. You will learn how your experiences shape who you are. It is my hope that this book will ignite a fire inside of you to become a better person.

CHAPTER 1
DO YOU KNOW WHO YOU ARE?

"A people without the knowledge of their past history, origin and culture is like a tree without roots."

–Marcus Garvey

Have you ever wondered who you are? Some answer that question by saying, "I am a child of God." Hardly anyone will say that they are the universe. We are made of atoms and molecules that are present in all things. The famous Deepak says, "A baby is born knowing that it is love and is completely lovable." We forget that as we grow and get accustomed to common practices in the world in which we live. Love is energy and we are energy. Yes we are love. People will also say we are spirit and that is true. Spirit is energy. The Merriam dictionary defines energy as......

Energy:

> Ability to be active: the physical or mental strength that allows you to do things.

Think about this; knowing we are energy means we are powerful beings and knowing how to use that energy can make all the difference in our lives. Energy is what we think, say and feel. The great thing about energy is that it can be controlled or manipulated. Energy is put into every intention that we have and that energy goes out into the universe with that intent in purpose.

Understanding that we are purely energy (spirit) is the key that will unlock how we are to operate in this universe. It is also a powerful awakening.

Learning about my culture has been a huge step in my continued growth as a person. Let's face it(comma) we as African Americans have been so far separated from learning about who we are and our roots. In school during black history month you learn about Harriet Tubman, Dr. Martin Luther King and Rosa Parks. Don't get me wrong, they are an important part of our history and definitely made huge strides in America. However, we need to know where we came from. Who were we before we became slaves? Who were we before our ancestors were captured and brought to America? There is a reason why our spirituality, language and practices were ripped away from us. If you have no sense of who you are, you can be easily controlled. It was imperative for slave masters to do this in order to control us.

One of the negatives of Christianity is that it has hindered us from learning who we are and it still does today. It definitely is not done by accident, it was done by design. Now I know some churches during black history month will have an African day and everyone comes dressed in their African attire like a costume party. That is how far it will go. We as African Americans have been scared to learn about our own culture so we reject it. It is frowned upon by many African Americans.

Henry Louis Gates said, "Africa is the mother of civilization itself...we have our roots here. And until we know Africa, we can never truly know ourselves." That is why we have so many issues within the black community because we are lost and searching. Knowing who you are and where you come from gives you a sense of pride. You will stand taller and want to make your Ancestors proud by taking all they have given you and doing something good with it. There is power in knowing who (you) are. People always talk about black on black crime but never talk about where black on black crime stems from. It comes from being lost of who we are. There are rippling effects that come from slavery and institutionalized racism and those effects are passed down from generation to generation. Dr. Joy Leary talks about Post Traumatic Slave Syndrome in her book and she also has a part 2 to that book called, "Be the Healing." I highly recommend reading those books.

Our people truly need healing and that starts by understanding who we are and what has been done to us and what is continuously being done to us.

It is imperative to take every opportunity to learn about your culture. Read as much as you can and participate in activities that teach cultural awareness. We have to teach our children that there is more to our history than what we learn in school. So now you know that you are spirit and that your Ancestors were a powerful people, they weren't just slaves. That is something to be proud of and once you embrace that, it makes you more beautiful beyond looks.

Many of us are defined by how successful we are, how much money we have, what we have, and how many degrees we have. Those things do not define who you are. I don't care if you are one of those very intelligent individuals with five degrees. If you do not know who you are, you have nothing. Knowing yourself is wisdom. Aristotle said, "Knowing yourself is the beginning of all wisdom."

We need to understand that there is no other me or you in this Universe. You were tailor made with your own individual purpose. You must know that! No I didn't say believe that but KNOW that. There is a huge difference in believing and knowing. Believing is accepting what someone told you as truth. Knowing is having knowledge in mastering something that you personally experienced.

CHAPTER 2
PERCEPTION

We see things from the distance we have traveled.

– Oyin

"Everything that has happened to you, you can either feel sorry for yourself or treat what happened to you as a gift. Everything is either an opportunity to grow or an obstacle to keep you from growing. You get to choose." This is one of the first quotes I heard from Dr. Wayne Dyer. I was at work listening to some of his lectures and when he spoke those words it hit me. I immediately understood that everything that happens to us good and bad are lessons for us in our lives. As soon as you find out what that lesson is, the situation doesn't seem as bad as we once perceived it to be. As a matter of fact, you will find that once you get the lesson that situation is forever changed.

As we move on in life we have to become familiar with the struggle between our spirit and our personality. It can be a struggle, but not if you constantly remind yourself that you are spirit. Our body is really just a shell that carries who we really are. It will die and turn into dust but we are eternal. This simply means that we have to start viewing things from who we really are, which is spirit. We have to stop looking at life through our personality. Our personalities are nothing but who we are based on emotions. Some call it "your ego self." When you look at things through the eyes of spirit you begin to see things that were never there before. You will see opportunities and ways to get out of bad situations. Spirit will tell you why a person acts as he/she does and you will stop getting upset about things you once did. Changing the way you see things will change your life. We know and understand that the sun rises and it falls. Now if we were to go up into space and look at the sun from a different view; we will see that the sun shines all the time. See how our perception changes things?

The amazing thing about perception is that we all have different perceptions. All of our perceptions are based on our mindsets, which are based on our experiences. Even if we are seeing with spirit, our awareness can be the same but our perceptions will be different. Some people may like the way a rose smells and someone else may think a rose stinks even though they both can smell the rose. Our perceptions may not always be the same and that is just fine. Always respect others perspectives. I personally love being around people who do not think the same as I do. I love hearing different opinions of others. Everyone has something unique to bring and others can point out things you would have never thought of. There is beauty when we can all harmonize our differences.

I used to love that quote, "It is what it is!" That was my motto. It was the perfect answer to everything that would pop up in my life. I would even tell other people, it is what it is and they would say, "You sure are right!" That quote has to be the biggest illusion there is. Of course when something happens, it definitely happened and you can't deny that. It is what it is, but it will become what you make of it. It will be exactly what you think it is. It is all about perception. You will not be able to always control certain situations in your life, but when problems arise you can always choose how to respond to it. How you handle situations will make all the difference in the world. Today I challenge you to change the way you look at things. Go deeper and find the good in some unpleasant situations. It is all about perception.

CHAPTER 3
THOUGHTS

What you think about today creates your tomorrow.

- Oyin

Scientists have discovered that our thoughts are power. Neuroscientists write about neuroplasticity and quantum physics all the time now. They have proven that our brains have the ability to change our synaptic wiring just from our thoughts. John Assaraf said, "Our thoughts not only matter, they create matter." It's energy. I(comma) like most people would always think of what I don't want to happen and what I don't want instead of what I want. In doing that, I manifest all the things I didn't want to happen in my life.

Conscious awareness and intention are vital to controlling your thoughts. You have to be aware of what you are thinking, aware of the moment, and aware of your surroundings. If you are not aware of your thoughts you can think negatively and not even know you are thinking negative thoughts. By doing this, you will create negative experiences in your life. It is important to exercise your mind daily. You may need to do it numerous times during the day. In your journal, make a list of your negative thoughts that you have repeatedly and your positive thoughts. Look them over and be aware of them. I like to listen to affirmations in the morning and at night. Lately, I have enjoyed listening to jazz because there are no words, just the sounds of instruments that give me happy thoughts. Doing these exercises empowers your mind. Also, add a mission statement or motto to your life. As you meditate, repeat it in your mind and then repeat out loud. You can do this while at work, school, or wherever you need to relax your mind and counter negative thoughts.

Of course bad experiences are going to happen in our lives. Every day will not be great, but it's all about how we handle it.

It is really that simple. What we think manifests. The Universe doesn't care if it's positive or negative; it brings us what it heard. Thoughts are more powerful than words. Don't get me wrong; what you say has power as well. If you align your thoughts with what you say it is like igniting dynamite. So if you think negative thoughts and say negative things to match those thoughts you will ignite nothing but negativity in your life. If you think positive thoughts and say positive things to match those thoughts you will ignite nothing but positivity in your life.

What we see and hear has an impact on our thoughts. Movies, books, television, music, and people all make impressions in what we think subconsciously. Therefore, it's important to filter what we let in our space, even people. Understand this, you do not have to process everything. You are in control of your thoughts and only you. Today I challenge you to take control of your thoughts. When you know it, you will see it.

CHAPTER 4
INTENTIONS

Intentions good and bad are the ingredients you give the Universe to create your reality.

–Oyin

In order to insure that the Universe gives you the things you want in life; always make sure everything you say and do come from good intentions. That means never do things in spite, anger, and frustration. You have to make sure that you always operate from love.

You have to love what you do. When you love what you do everything just falls in place. When you are happy and at peace, you are emitting love into the Universe. Consequently, the Universe has no choice but to bring the same back to you. Operating from fear will only take you further away from where you want to be in life. People who operate from fear with the intentions of using people to get ahead for money or fame may do so, but it will come with a price. The Universe will reciprocate the same energy you are putting out. That person could become very successful and end up hurt by someone who used them the same way they did the people/person before. Intentions are so important.

So often I would operate from fear in my life. We all do it and have done it. I would do things for people not because I loved them and wanted to make them happy; I would do things to be accepted and loved. I remember when I was in a relationship with my daughter's father. He cheated on me and was just so disrespectful to me. Deep down I knew I shouldn't have accepted that behavior and as crazy as it sounds; I felt if I just stayed that God would see me trying and would work things out. I knew God would make him love me all the more. I felt a good woman who cooked, washed his clothes, and did nice things, it would show that I deserved the love I needed. All these things I did just knowing it would make him happy and he would get his act together, and magically this happy family I had envisioned would appear. The only thing that came out of that was more heartache and pain. I can even remember being mad at God because I knew I was good to this man and did everything in my power to prove that. I look back at that time in my life and laugh now because I was so lost! The problem with what I did is, I didn't love myself enough to know that I deserved better and my intentions were all wrong. I did all those things because I was scared he would leave me to raise a child alone. Everything I did was based on fear.

Since I operated from fear the Universe gave me everything I feared. I ended up raising my daughter alone. It was all on me just as I feared.

The best way to make sure that my intentions are coming from love; I do things without any expectations from the other person. If I let my ego get in the way, and feel like I really don't want to do it. When someone does or says something; I have learned not to react. If someone invites me somewhere and I really feel like I don't want to go, I have learned to not make myself go. I don't go because I will not be in a good mood. That type of energy will be felt by others, and I would be emitting that energy into the Universe. If I am doing something for someone hoping they will do the same for me in return, I try my best not to do it. I want to do things for people simply because I love them and just want to help them. There are times I just want to put a smile on someone's face. That is the type of energy you want to send out in the Universe.

In church we were taught, "What you sow is what you reap." It's the same as what you put out in the Universe, is what you will get back. Now we all know about Karma. You do something bad to someone and in your mind you have already told yourself; "I know all the wrong I've done will come back to me one day". You do not have to be a victim of Karma. If you can own up to your mistakes and redirect it by making those mistakes right, you can redirect Karma. If it's a person you hurt, go to them and make it right. Apologize with sincerity and ask how you can make what you did right,(then) you will redirect Karma. If someone has hurt you, do not wish that their lives will be miserable. Pray that God will show them how wrong they were and let it go. If you seek revenge or hope that their life will be miserable, the Universe will give you what you put out. That old saying is true," When you dig a grave for someone else dig two, one for them and one for you." You will never be able to control how someone may treat you, but you can control how you react. How you react to it will control that situation. If you see or hear about a person that has done you wrong, and they are doing miserably, never say, "That's what that fool gets!" Pray that God will bring them out of it. I know it can be hard to do, but the more you get into a practice of doing this you will see how blessed your life will be. You will not want to wish bad on anyone ever again.

Our intentions are so powerful; I can't say it enough. When you are mindful of your intentions, and you are operating out of love you will have no regrets. I challenge you today to write down your goals and analyze your intentions with each goal you note. The ball is always in your court.

CHAPTER 5
LETTING IT GO

Letting go removes fear.

- Oyin

Letting go can be very difficult; it truly takes practice. I struggle with it more so with situations and experiences that are close to me. You have heard the saying, "Let it go and let it flow." You really cannot move forward in life until you let things go. Holding onto pain, anger, and regret truly weighs you down. We hear people say these things all the time but a lot of us just don't know how to let go.

There are a plethora of ways and steps of letting go but the one I find most helpful is to cry. Yes cry! Crying is good for the soul. Neuroscientist Dr. William H Frey II, PhD., stated that crying..

Lowers your blood pressure, pulse and body immediately
Removes toxins that build up from stress
85% of women and 73% of men felt less sad and angry after crying

So go ahead and cry. Get it all out. After crying, write down your feelings in a journal. Write about what you learned from any painful experiences. Relationships with friends and romantic relationships are truly hard to let go of. Years ago I was in a somewhat romantic relationship and it lasted about 3 years. We started out as great friends, we would spend the weekends together, go on short trips and he spoiled me with gifts. Anything I mentioned that I liked he would get it for me. We were never an official couple. I wanted a true loving romantic relationship and for him to say," that's my woman". He never would. Now keep in mind, that we spent all this time together. He finally told me one day that he didn't like that I was overweight. That was devastating to me. It really hit my self-esteem. I felt and believed that I was ugly and undesirable. He eventually went on with his life and I was truly hurt by that experience. No one has ever hurt me that way in my life. I immediately went into a state of depression. I was miserable. All I could think about was how ugly I was. I felt that three years of my life were a complete waste of time. Deep down I knew I wasn't ugly, see our emotions will take us so far from the truth. I really had to wrestle with what happened to me, and I did that by separating what was truth and what was emotion. I had to look at that experience and look at what it taught me; what good came out of it and then it was time for me to let it go. The truth out of that experience was that yes I am fat; I do need to do something about it. He enjoyed me as a person and I had some great times with him. I went to places I have never been and I enjoyed that. I also had to put myself in his shoes. If I was searching for something and couldn't find my happiness there, I would want to move on. I had to realize that I wasn't meant for him and he wasn't meant for me. That wasn't a bad thing, it was a good thing. I wouldn't be where I am now, and never would have had some very dear people in my life if I had been with him. I had to humanize him. Laura Oliver has a great quote, "It's better letting go of a human than a hero."

When it comes to friendships and just people in general, there are times when we get offended about a particular situation or we offend someone. A lot of friendships end because of some of the craziest things. We will quickly say, "I'm not talking to that person ever again." As I continue to grow and mature in life I find that putting myself in the other person's shoes who offended me; that helps me to understand them better. If I offended someone I can sit back and think to myself what could I have said or done differently in this situation. By doing that you are taking responsibility of the matter and less likely to get angry and say something awful and make the situation worse. If someone offends you or you offend them, go to them and talk after you have cooled off and make sure your words are kind and sincere. Let them know how you feel if they offended you. If you offended them let them know you understand, and respect how they feel and offer your sincerest apology.

It is amazing that I like people I once didn't now that I have dealt with my own issues. People will say that they don't like a certain person, but reality is the people we don't like are really an extension of who we are. They remind us of something we don't like within ourselves. You know that person that just irritates you for no reason. Do some self-reflection and you will find it's something within you, not them. Learn to let that kind of stuff go. Get it out of your life because it will hinder your growth. Remember the Universe hears your thoughts before you do.

Letting go is vital to your health. It's important to have good people around you that you can call to vent, cry on, and laugh together. Laughing is such a great release. Whenever you find yourself stressed go watch a funny comedy, get with your buddies and go exercise, or focus on that project you have wanted to do or finish. Replace anger and pain with helping someone else; volunteer in the community and focus on helping others. It is a great way to move forward.

You also have to learn to let go of worrying about what people say about you. People are going to say things about you good and bad. You cannot allow yourself to be a prisoner of what someone else thinks about you. To be honest, it's none of your business what others are saying about you. It is so easy to get caught up into seeking approval from others by their compliments or dislikes. It is nice when someone compliments you but never let it go to your head. You have to find encouragement and acknowledgement within yourself. If you are always seeking others approval by looking for compliments then how will you act when the compliments stop coming? Always be secure in who you are. Now it's good to have a friend who can tell you the truth. Look at the show American Idol; those kids who try out for that show can't sing at all. They get on TV looking ridiculous because no one had the heart to tell them they can't sing, but they definitely had confidence. Lol. We need that friend to keep us from looking like a fool.

Letting go is forgiveness. We have to forgive those who have wronged us in life in order to enjoy our lives. Forgiving others is not necessarily for them but for us. It will bring you peace. Also, you have to forgive yourself for any regrets or mistakes you have made in your life. You cannot focus on the past or the future, but only NOW in the present moment. Your soul is not in the past; your soul is not in the future. Your soul is in the present moment. You need to be aligned with your soul at all times. When you are aligned with your soul everything you do is powerful and in your purpose.

CHAPTER 6
SPIRITUALITY

Spirituality is when you understand that
the voice within is you.

– Oyin

As a child I grew up as an African
Methodist in Philadelphia, Pennsylvania.
Later on when my family moved to Tulsa,
Oklahoma we became Baptists. Then it
was on to a non-denominational church
and that is the faith I kept into my adult
life and my children's until later. In Tulsa,
I attended Higher Dimensions led by
Bishop Carlton Pearson. We lovingly
called it, Higher D and we called Carlton
Pearson, "Bishop." I loved that church!
My kids were excited to go every Sunday.
It was so awesome and spiritual. I lived in
North Tulsa, Turley to be exact and
Higher Dimensions was way out in South

Tulsa. It was a drive! I would make that drive every Sunday. I admired Bishop Carlton Pearson because he was genuine and whenever I spoke to him, even though it was always just a brief few seconds he made me feel loved. A hug from him made you feel as though you had a spiritual conversation. I was in awe by that and wanted to always leave that impression with anyone I met. People would always say that only the black folks with money go to Higher D. That was so far from the truth because I would scrape up change out the couch some days to just have gas money to drive out there. Matter of fact, I think my car was one of the most raggedy ones in the parking lot. I had a Chevy Beretta with no A/C, only one window would roll down and two hubcaps. We had to pray before we got into that car to safely make it to our destinations. Bishop started preaching about The Gospel of Inclusion. The Gospel of Inclusion taught that God loves everyone no matter who you are or what you did. The Gospel of Inclusion taught that God is not an angry God sending people to hell. Members started going crazy! Eventually, members would start to leave and each Sunday the congregation would get smaller and smaller. I stayed until the last day. I so understood, the message Bishop was teaching. People thought I was insane by continuing to attend Higher Dimensions. People would actually stop talking to me when they found out I was attending Higher D and holidays with family became debates about Higher D, Bishop and what the Bible says. I remember watching people who Bishop helped just walk away from him. That dreadful day came when Bishop closed the doors to Higher Dimensions and moved to Chicago. Never will I forget Bishop's last sermon at Higher D and I can see him now singing Sam Cooke's song, "A Change Gonna Come." I felt lost. The feeling came over me that I had when my parents told me they were getting a divorce. Bishop gave me my first introduction to my spirit and to consciousness. There was no place that fit for me after that. I would visit different churches here and there and then I settled at World Won for Christ. I loved that church as well and Pastor Melvin Cooper but I always sat there feeling like I was just going through the motions of church. I was searching for something more fulfilling; so I started to get involved in the community by volunteering my time to get people registered to vote and working with others to get Greenwood in The National Historic Register. While out in the community, I was reunited with my cousin Chief. Chief always embraced African culture and taught others about African Culture and I started listening and learning and getting my kids involved in their culture. I loved being around Chief because his spirit was so inviting and it reminded me of how I felt when I was at

Higher Dimensions. Through Chief I learned about Yoruba culture and an African spirituality system called Ifa which means, "God's Consciousness". It was somewhat like the Gospel of Inclusion to me that I learned from Carlton Pearson but more. The more I learned and experienced, I understood why our spirituality was stripped from us when we were enslaved. I realized how much was taken from our Ancestors spirituality and twisted into Christianity. Eventually, I became an Ifa devotee. Shortly after that, I went through Chief's rebirth class which is a weekend of nothing but learning affirmations, meditation, and understanding spirit. You go in on a Friday evening and you have to wear all white clothing. All you can have is a pen and journal. No laptop or phones. That was the hardest part for me! I couldn't be away from my phone for 10 minutes and I couldn't imagine being away from my phone for an entire weekend. Rebirth is Friday through Sunday. It is a lot of book work and listening; It's really class. You stay in one room the entire weekend. You can come out to go to the bathroom and shower. Food will only consist of fruits, vegetables, tea and water which are all provided for you. At the end of Rebirth you are given a ceremony with all your favorite foods with family and friends. I came out of that rebirth retreat a totally different person. I started meditating on a daily basis and just absorbing the knowledge I was taught and I continued on my own to read and just get more and more knowledge, and then I started slowly applying what I was learning to my life. In Ifa, you get what is called a head reading which is like your life story that is documented and defined for you by spirit. When I received my head reading which came from Africa, everything just started changing day by day. I was open and eager to see what each day would bring and I would really try to learn from each experience. As time passed on, I started to feel like I needed more time alone. I started to spend more time with myself and just applying everything I was learning and taught throughout my life. My alone time allowed me to get acquainted with the new me that I was becoming. A few months later, I started to attract people in my life who would bring things I had prayed for, or they would bring things I needed in my life. There were not just material things but love and knowledge. I started to become really aware of how my spirit would attract people and wonderful things to me. My life just started changing for the better. Even my view on politics changed once I stopped believing in God and started knowing God. The way I viewed people changed. I started to see everyone as a spirit and not human. Chief always says, "We are spirit having human experiences." I believe that there are many paths to the mountain. Which one you take is not for me to judge, but I do know it is very important to be in touch with your spirit. You cannot love yourself and love someone else until you discover that connection with God and your spirit. When you find that connection you become one with God. Funny thing is, that I always thought I had that connection. I didn't! It took me all this time to understand that. Now I can look at myself in the mirror and see God. Bishop was absolutely right when he sang that song at our last day at Higher D; "Change is Gonna." It did, for him and me! The City that once rejected him has embraced him again. Yes, he still has some haters but he is back in Tulsa doing wonderful things. I still go see him from time to time at All Souls and I love listening to his web show called, "Streaming Consciousness." It's so ironic, because now everyone loves to watch Oprah's Super Soul Sunday and see all the progressive spiritual leaders that talk about consciousness. Bishop introduced that to Tulsa many years before. The only thing I regret during that time of my life I spent at Higher D was; that I never had a real conversation with Bishop. My favorite seat was in the back left corner at Higher D, and I never mingled much except for when I would see my friend Moochie who was just like an Aunt to me. I really do regret not knowing Bishop the way others did but I do know we were acquainted through spirit. God has a way of giving us just what we need. What I learned from Bishop is that when you find truth about who you are, embrace it. People will talk about you and you will lose many people, but you have to stay focused and continue on your purpose. I will never forget Bishop talking to us about people being bridges. Bridges help get people to their destinations; and what happens to bridges? They get stepped on constantly but the bridge is strong and can handle a lot of weight. I know those are not his exact words, but that is the way I remember that lesson.

CHAPTER 7
POLITICS

Politics will test your character, spirit and morals all at the same time.

- Oyin

I have always loved politics. Since I was just a little girl I wanted to be a Senator. It was me who always wanted to help the underdog. My father was always a leader. He was the president of the neighborhood association and on various boards throughout my life. I always admired his wit and strength to lead people and defend people who were wronged.

Chief and I would get involved in many things in the community but Chief always operated from a spiritual stand point. He was never too much into politics but more into what is right. Before I founded Ifa, I was that militant pro black life person. My family used to call me the militant midget after the character Michael in that old television show, "Good Times." Actually, my cousin Angie started that. I was angry about how Africans were treated globally, and particularly how we were treated in America. I would snap off at anyone who dare tried me no matter what setting I was in. I meant well but I was a mess.

Once I found Ifa I started to change. My entire view concerning politics was changing. Seeing people as spirit and not being so judgmental truly changed who I have become. Meetings and being at certain events seem to not matter to me as much and I believe it was because I was finding myself; and that is where my focus was. Ifa truly humbled me and it didn't happen overnight. I know some people who know me will say, "Kristi does not have it all together." No, I do not have it all together and I don't know everything. I am learning, loving, maturing, and constantly evolving. There are many days when I was not the same person I was yesterday. Each day I get to learn something new about the new me. I truly die daily.

I do believe that if we are to be successful in life that we have to give back our time in the community. We also have to be involved locally and nationally in government by understanding the voting process, social issues, and be active in ways to make them better. You may not ever run for office but support someone who is running for office that shares your ideas. Serving others is so huge. It is a must for us to serve others. We have so many issues within our community and a big part of that is, we as a people do not care to know what is going on in the community. We don't care to know what the officials who govern our communities are doing. You cannot be a parent and think that it's okay to just raise your kids and have a nice car and a house. It's more to it than that. You have to teach your children the importance of community and that it's our responsibility to build up our communities. Some people start to make a lot of money and move away from the community they used to live in, get a big house, and a big fence to keep people out. I read somewhere a long time ago that when you start to make a lot of money, you don't go and buy a bigger fence, you buy a bigger table. Teach your children to be aware of what is going on in their community, city, state and the world they live in.

As I said early on, Ifa has humbled me. I now see people as spirit and see other politicians who I once could not stand as spirit. Republican or Democrat, I don't see that anymore; I see spirit. To be a leader you really have to learn to be humble and have humility. Humility is one of the hardest things I had to learn and I still struggle with it at times. I was always that no nonsense person who had to tell someone off if I felt offended by something, or just loving the need to be that bad ass. I had to teach people to not ever mess with me especially when it came to politics. Little did I know that by demonstrating humility it opened the gates of the Universe to me and great opportunities.

Lao Tzu said, "All streams flow to the sea because it is lower than they are. Humility gives it it's power. If you want to govern the people, you must place yourself below them. If you want to lead the people, you must learn how to follow them."

Every politician or aspiring politician needs to memorize that quote. I challenge you today to demonstrate humility when a situation arises. The more you practice it, the easier it will become. Try it, I dare you.

CHAPTER 8
ATTRACTION

What you say and think over and over in your mind is what you will attract.

– Oyin

Over the years and watching Oprah's Super Soul Sunday we have all heard about the Law of Attraction. Well it is the truth! I always hear people say, "I am tired of hearing that!" Well get used to it if you want to change your life. It is the gospel of life. You are what you attract.

You may think about a bad relationship you were in or are in now and say," I didn't attract that mess in my life". I guarantee you that 90% of the time you did. You attracted it into your life by your thoughts or intentions. Yes people will come into your life and you look up and think to yourself," where in the world did this awful person come from?" Often time's people will come in your life simply because they are attracted to your light. Think about those summer nights when the porch light is on; it attracts moths and those annoying bugs that make that awful noise. That's how your light works. People will be attracted to your light and they are a lesson for you or you may be the lesson for them. Some will get what they need and leave and others will stay in your life.

While learning to control your thoughts be mindful, be in tune with your spirit, and operate from love which are the ingredients you need to attract good people, great opportunities, prosperity, and love into your life. You determine your outcome.

Years ago when the book, "The Law of Attraction" came out, people were all over it. They wanted to attract money into their lives. Well you definitely can attract money. I have learned to have the attitude to stop worrying about not having enough money to pay this or to do that. As a single mother I know first-hand how money can stress you out. Especially having a child in sports who plays all year round, it can get expensive. You constantly feel the burden of making things stretch and robbing Peter to pay Paul. There were many times I would go to the casino with the intentions on getting money to pay something and that is definitely the wrong thing to do! I had to learn to change my perception about money. In the mornings when I get up I take some time to myself to mediate and thank God for allowing me to have another day. I make a habit to say thank you for what I have, thank you for supplying me with what I need, thank you for blessing me to able to help others, and thank you for blessing me with what I want. It starts me off in a good place. On days where I do start to worry about money, I immediately thank God for supplying my needs and helping me through it. It always works out for me when I do that. Even today I have been blessed with opportunities to help me and put me at a better place in my life. You have to know that God doesn't want you to struggle in life and you have the power not to. Now I am not promising you that you can be a billionaire but I do know if you put your mind to it, and if it is in your purpose you can achieve whatever you want.

CHAPTER 9
SEX

Sex is spiritual whether you know it or
not.

- Oyin

Our society today has such a warped sense
of sex. It is commercialized in everything
from music, movies, and television
commercials. It is so casual. I don't think I
need to go into how many diseases that are
out there besides HIV. No one talks about
the damage that having casual sex can
cause. Having sex with the wrong person
is just as damaging as any disease that can
attack your body physically. As parents
we talk to our children about the birds and
the bees, birth control, and abstinence. We
are not telling them about what happens to
them spiritually.

First, let's understand that sex is a spiritual ritual. A woman's vagina is a sacred place in which life passes. It is a sacred place where souls intertwine, spiritual energy is left and taken. When you have sex with someone you literally have sex with everyone that person has had sex with. That means you also take in all that spiritual energy from the people your partner has had sex with. Your soul is saying, "Who are all these people?" That energy stays with you and it does impact your life. That applies to males and females. It is important to really get to know someone before you decide to let them in your sacred place. Understand who you are, you are not just human. You are spirit having human experiences; you have to protect your spirit.

Women get attached emotionally from having sex with someone and that is because we carry the portal in which life passes. I hear guys complain all the time after they have had sex with a woman about how she got caught up in her feelings. Men have no idea that they have joined her in a spiritual ritual. We are not taught that. All our lives, especially those who grew up in church, we were told not to have a sex until marriage because it is a sin. No one ever explained what really goes on when you have sex.

Women it is so important to understand the power you have and not just with sex, but your feminine energy. Chief taught me this Yoruba Odu that says, "A woman has the power to make a beggar a King and a King a beggar." Feminine energy is the most powerful energy there is.

You can use stories that we were all taught from the Bible. Samson lost his power to Delilah. Let's not forget Solomon and David. We as women must understand this and we need to teach that to our sons as well. Young adult males seem to always be taught something different when it comes to relationships and sex. We teach them differently than we do our girls and that's understandable. I can truly see the differences, but mothers we have to teach our young men to be careful with the hearts of women and how to respect them. We actually teach them that by how we allow men in our lives to treat us.

CHAPTER 10
PRAYER & MEDITATION

Prayer and meditation is nothing but a
conversation with God.

– Oyin

Simply put, prayer is when you talk to
God and meditation is when God talks to
you. You cannot grow spiritually if you
are not meditating on a consistent basis.
Learning to balance your emotions only
comes from meditation. I don't care how
long you have been in church, if you go
every Sunday and Wednesday, what your
rank is in your spiritual or religious
entities. If you are not meditating on a
consistent basis I can promise you that
you are not allowing your spirit to grow.
Now I know that if you go around talking
about meditation to church folk, they will
look at you crazy. African Americans
have totally rejected our Ancestors
spirituality and there is so much we are

missing out on. Church will not teach you about meditating and how to meditate. Even in the Bible it talks about meditation. In the Old Testament Isaac went out into the fields to meditate. Genesis Chapter 24:63 says, "And he went out into the field one evening to meditate and as he looked up, he saw camels approaching". There are other examples but I will not go through them all because this isn't that kind of book.

I have heard people say many times, "the soul knows what it needs to heal itself". The challenge is to silence the mind. Meditation is so important. It is like an exercise that strengthens a muscle. I like to pray during my mediation. I get in a quiet place which is usually lying in my bed on my back or sitting up in my bed just looking out of my window. I use that time to pray for people, pray for myself, and speak to my Ancestors. I thank God and my Ancestors for helping me and then

I just get quiet so I can hear God speak to me. I have a visual of my back yard, meaning I can tell you where the trees are and etc. When I started meditating while looking out my bedroom window, I can tell you the marks on the trees, the day the leaves began to turn color, and what kind of birds that frequent my backyard. Meditation makes you look deeper at things. There are mediation guides I use on YouTube from Dr. Wayne Dyer and Deepak that I love. I plug in my headphones and just let spirit take me. If you are starting out with meditation those are some really good meditation guides for you to start with. Throughout the day you can meditate. Meditation can last from 5 minutes to hours. You may meditate at your desk when you have a few moments or walking from your car into a building. Whenever I get stressed at work and have to meet deadlines, I take a few minutes to silence my mind and have a conversation with God. When I do that, ideas come to me that make the tasks easier. Again, this is a very important practice to do in your life. Going through life committed to your spiritual or religious practices and not meditating is like planning to lose weight without any exercise. You will not get the results you are looking for.

Prayer is also important. In Christianity there are angels, in African Spirituality there are Ancestors. Christianity teaches that God will send Angels to come and help you. African Spirituality teaches that God sends your Ancestors to help you. So when I pray I also talk to my Ancestors. I will not go any deeper than that because my goal is to just get you to understand how important prayer is. When we pray it is important to not always make it about us. God knows what we need before we even ask. However, it's powerful to take time out of your day to pray for someone else and just express gratitude by simply saying, thank you. Now here is the part about prayer that we often forget. We do not act after we pray. After you pray you have to know that your prayer was answered and act accordingly. There is an African Proverb that says, "When you pray move your feet." You have to exercise faith which is relying on spirit. Trust that God will give you what you need to see it through.

I challenge you to start meditating and use the guides from Krs One, Dr. Wayne Dyer, and Deepak. You can search them on YouTube and get some of their books.

CHAPTER 11
KNOWLEDGE

Knowledge is not meant to sit on.

- Oyin

We live in the age of computers. Everything we may have ever wanted to know is at our fingertips. Almost everything in this book was knowledge that was given to me, researched, and that I learned through experience. I am blessed that I have people in my life who have taken time out of their lives to share their knowledge with me. It is a beautiful thing when people come into our lives and see something in you that you didn't see in yourself. As my cousin Chief says, "Some people will look on the ground and see a caterpillar and some will see a butterfly." Those people are so patient, loving and caring and, they are molding you and you don't even know it. When I went into rebirth class with Chief for a weekend there was so much information that I learned. Rebirth goes into depth about spirit, meditation, God, and that oneness with God. It was book work, it was spiritual work, and it was homework. I remember thinking to myself on the last night of Rebirth classes, "How in the world can a person go through this and not be changed?" After rebirth I wanted to know more and more. I completely turned into a sponge. I even unknowingly distanced myself a lot from everyone because I just wanted to absorb all that I could. Through rebirth I was introduced to Deepak Chopra's work, so I started reading all about him. I listened to his lectures on YouTube, and then I accidentally heard a lecture from Dr. Wayne Dyer. Well that was no accident. Then I started to read about James Weeks who produced Across the King's River and I began soaking up everything I possibly could. It's like I wanted to catch up on everything I had been missing. I wrestled so much with my ego because I was looking at everyone around me; especially those in my circle. I was thinking to myself, "How can you not want to read and know all this stuff I am finding out about?" I would quickly learn that what I was doing is judging others, and just needed to focus on getting myself together. None of us are perfect and that included me. After I started absorbing all this information I decided to put it to work. I began to see how much it worked for me and I even felt magical at times. I felt as if my brain was a wand or I was becoming like the character in that movie, "Lucy". I laugh at myself writing that because I was amazed at how powerful we really are. It's one thing when someone tells you that and you believe it, but it's another thing when someone tells you that and you experience it. Once you experience it, you know it. What that did for me was make me realize that as a parent, I need to put into action what I was learning so I can teach my children. It's like sending your kids to church and you don't even go. Your kids come home from learning how to live morally, and you as the parent are not being an example of what you are sending them to church to learn. Children learn by what they see you do, not what you tell them. I really want my children to look at me and see the changes I have made and see me utilizing knowledge that I have learned. I can tell my kids how to meditate, how to get through tough times, and talk about the ups and downs of life. I will say this again, I am not perfect. I make mistakes all the time but it's about owning up to those mistakes and learning from them. I have to be that living example not only to my children, but for other people around me. When I see my loved ones hurting, I want to be able to offer advice that can really help them with the knowledge I have applied to my life.

You owe it to yourself to always gain knowledge. The body isn't the only thing that needs nourishment. Nurture your soul by expanding your consciousness through reading and learning. Apply the knowledge you have learned and share it with others. It is an insult to the person who has taken time out of their lives to teach you knowledge and you do nothing with it.

I have many favorite quotes but if I had to do a top five; I would put this quote from Mark Twain at number 3 on the list. Mark Twain says, "I have never let my schooling interfere with my education." Experience is your education. I challenge you today to take some time out of your week and pick a book to read that will expand your consciousness.

CHAPTER 12
PEOPLE

Be the type of person you want to meet.

- Oyin

I can understand why monks seclude themselves away from the world. The world is definitely a distraction to your spiritual life, but we have to learn how to coexist with people who do not have the same beliefs, respect and manners as we do. We live in a world where we cannot expect people to react as we would or like the same things that we like.

Everyone that you meet in your life is a teacher. If you truly observe, everyone has something to teach you and everyone knows something that you do not know. There are days that I don't want to be bothered with people period. Then I have days where I want to get out and just love on people and chit chat. I'm the type of person that doesn't necessarily have to know a person before I can have a conversation with them. It used to be challenging for me to deal with a bunch of different personalities and sometimes it still is. There are some people who will come into your life that you just gel with. It's a synergy that takes place, and some people you will not have that connection with and that's okay. Still show love and respect for them.

I learned a very good lesson when I was in the hospital after I had my surgery. There were so many people who took time out of their busy schedules to come see me at the hospital and to come see me once I came home. People called and checked on me, and asked if I needed anything. I would say, "No I'm good and thank you." Some people who I told that I was okay and didn't need anything would still come by and bring me food and other things. They even offered to help pick up my son from games and go to his games since I couldn't be there to cheer him on. I didn't have to worry about cooking for a good while. People came by who I didn't even talk to on a regular basis or haven't talked to in years. I was truly humbled, and I was more humbled because people came to see me who I didn't make the time to go and see. I thought and prayed about them but I never adjusted my time to go and see them. That taught me such a great lesson. It not only taught me to be the kind of person I wanted others to be; it taught me the true meaning of what a community is supposed to do. I am not mad or upset about the people who never went out their way to come and visit me or bring me food. I learned a lot from those who did come to see me when I never took the time to go see them. I asked myself, "How can I say I love my friends and not be there for them?" It helped me to see that I needed to be a better friend and a better person period to those I called my friends.

People will always make time for what's important to them and I should have done that. I knew then that I needed to take a look at myself and edit myself throughout that entire experience. People can teach you lessons that will last a lifetime. It is up to us to get the lesson.

A lot of black people will see me with my friends who are not black and will ask me, "I thought you were Pan-Afrikan and talk all this pro-black stuff so why you have these white friends?" Even though I unapologetically embrace my culture and promote black pride by all means; I still have friends from all different races and backgrounds who I truly love and adore. They all bring not only joy to my life but they always uplift me and we respect and support each other's differences. We will do anything to help each other. Understanding that we are all spirit is key to relationships with others. Of course I can see the color of their skin and find beauty in their cultures but more importantly, I can see their spirit.

Another thing about people is that they will not always be kind. They will say awful things about you behind your back and be more into your business rather than their own. Remember it's all about how you react to it. I find that is better to let people talk but make sure you don't give them anything to talk about. Everyone isn't meant for you to talk to about your goals, dreams or even just to vent. There will be people who will not share in your happiness and do not care about whatever problems you may have. Some people are just nosey and will take your conversations back to other people. If someone has done you like that, do not share information with them again. Continue to be nice and courteous but proceed with caution.

CHAPTER 13
HEALTH

Good health is nothing but a natural
healer.

- Oyin

Taking care of our health seems like the
last thing anyone wants to do, specifically
African Americans. We do not like to visit
the doctor. The older we get the more
wear and tear on our bodies and we have
to start taking care of ourselves. Now a
days, people look for natural remedies for
healing their bodies and that is great.
However, once you have let health issues
go too long those natural remedies can't
do anything. So many of us carry health
insurance, dental, and vision insurance but
we do not use it.

Men and women should get their yearly
exams. I always say, "God made doctors

71

for a reason;" Use them. The dentist is one doctor that people hate more than their health physician. We all should visit them twice a year for cleanings and a checkup. Did you know that not getting your teeth clean can cause you to have heart disease? Bacteria get down into your gums and into the blood stream and can cause heart disease. Also, a dentist can look at your gums and tell if you have dementia, heart disease, and cancer.

I let three years go by without seeing a doctor. I was experiencing menstrual cycles that lasted 15 days, and were heavy and painful. As time went by I started to notice how tired I was and just didn't have the drive to do much but go to work and home. If I did anything else after work it really wore me to a point that I would be so weak. As more time went on I was getting worse; I could hear my pulse in my ear constantly. The fatigue was out of this world, and I noticed my skin would get really dry and my finger nails were always brittle. Then my hair started shedding a lot. I remember going to meetings and different functions and I would be so exhausted. I couldn't even serve food because at that point I was experiencing dizzy spells and everything looked like it would be spinning. When I would get up I would see little white dots all over. I kept all this to myself and just wrote it off in my mind. I would make the excuse to myself that I needed more rest and that I needed to probably eat more carbs because I went on a low carb diet. All this time my body was giving me signs and I kept ignoring them. Every day at work I would workout by climbing 14 flights of stairs. Each day instead of getting better and better, I would feel worse and worse. Three flights would make me feel as if I was going to pass out, but I kept pushing myself knowing that I was out of shape and just needed to push on. One night while I slept a voice said, "Kris you need to go to the doctor." I can still hear that voice today. Two days went by and that same voice would tell me at the same time each night that I need to go to the doctor. As I was at work I noticed that my schedule was busy so I was going to wait two weeks to go see the doctor. As soon as I had that thought I heard the voice again, "Kris you need to go to the doctor." I finally made the appointment with my OBGYN. As the nurse was taking my blood pressure, the machine beeped like it was broken. The beep was so loud. The nurse said, "This can't be right!" So she took it again. My blood pressure was fine but my heart rate was 126 which meant that my heart actually beat 126 times per minute which was very dangerous. My doctor gave me an exam and immediately came to the conclusion that I was severely anemic but needed to do blood work to back her suspicions. She also said my uterus was enlarged and suspected I had fibroids which was associated with the

long and heavy menstrual cycles. My
cousin chief did a ritual for me to Ogun
and Babaluaye for my health. The very
next day while I was at work, I received a
phone call from my doctor. Usually the
nurse calls but it was my actual doctor
which made me very nervous. She
informed me that I would need a blood
transfusion as soon as possible and that
my HCT levels were 4.8. My doctor said,
"I do not know how you are able to stand
up!" She stated that my heart is also over
compensating due to the lack of iron
which made it very hard for my red blood
cells to carry oxygen throughout my body.
My red blood cells were only carrying
17% of oxygen. I could have gone into
cardiac arrest going up those stairs and
had I waited to make the appointment;
there was a possibility that I could have
died. After the blood transfusion I felt a
lot better but came to find out I had 5 huge
fibroids in my uterus that were bleeding
and causing the anemia. I eventually had

to have a partial hysterectomy. Now if I had listened to my body early on I could have prevented myself from having a hysterectomy. It really wasn't a hard decision for me to make. I made sure that I had no other alternatives; it was the only choice I had if I wanted to survive. Gratitude immediately took over and I thanked God for blessing me with two children. I have a boy and girl and I know I would have been devastated if I didn't have any children, or wanted to have more children. Lately I have been telling women I know that if they have long heavy cycles and iron is low they need to get themselves checked out because it can become very serious. Some listen and some do not.

Your body wants to be healthy. The internet has so much information out there about natural healing, but it is also important to contact your doctor. If you don't like your doctor ask friends and family if they would recommend their doctor to you. I am not against the natural medicine route but I am for preventative care. It is so important that we stay on top of our health by eating right and exercising. We only get one body. In 2014 I started losing weight the slow and hard way. I started out at 209 pounds. The more I started loving myself the more I wanted to do better. Today I am 149 pounds. It took me one year to lose 60 pounds. Every now and then I look at the pictures of me when I weighed 209 pounds. I am only 4'11 so I was really an oompa loompa walking around. I was so unhappy with myself at that weight. A few months ago I was so proud of myself and I thought it was wrong to feel that way. I didn't want ego to control me but I really had accomplished something to be proud of. That was truly some hard work and I still have a ways to go. There is nothing wrong with encouraging yourself and patting yourself on the back sometimes.

When you take care of yourself, you feel better, and when you feel better the happier you are in life. So start listening to your body and do not be afraid to see your doctor. Today I challenge you to write down your weight goals and a plan on how to get there. If you just want to start eating healthy write that down and try to make small changes, then gradually work your way up to the bigger changes. I also challenge you to see your doctor about health issues that you may be experiencing; Stop putting it off.

CHAPTER 14
HUMILITY

Humility is saying no to pride and yes to spirit.

- Oyin

I was reading an article in The Huffington Post about humility. The article stated that most people today find humble people weak and unassertive. I found that to be interesting because when you really stop and think about a person who is humble, they are really strong individuals and powerful.

In my past, it didn't take me very long to get angry when I felt that someone attacked my pride. I didn't care if I was right or if I was wrong. I was going to let you have it for trying to make a fool out of me. Today I still have days where I let my pride get puffed up, but now I can stand back more often and edit myself. The first day I noticed that I was truly changing was through an incident on Facebook. Earlier that day at work, my coworkers and I were talking about married men having single women as friends. My co-worker was talking about how jealous she was of her husband's friend and their closeness. We all had different opinions about it and my opinion was that there is a line. Married women do not like their husbands being very close to other women. Later that night I decided to post about it on Facebook after reading the posts from other co-workers. I never expected the turn that post had taken. A couple close to me felt I was talking about them. They took it very personal and it was never about them. It got heated, I was angry, and hurt because they were attacking me and just ripping me on Facebook. It was so bad; people were calling me and in boxing me to see if everything was alright and wanted to know what happened. My coworkers were like, "What just happened?" I tried to explain what happened but it was like they were committed to misunderstanding me. I wanted to go off! I felt they made a fool of me and I was angry. I begin to type my last response and it was full of anger and madness. Right before I was ready to click "post" spirit said, "Don't send that," you explained yourself and that was enough." I went to lie in my bed and I actually had mad tears just rolling down my face. You know those mad tears when you are so angry you cry and your head starts hurting. My friend called me and we talked about that for hours. He said, "You didn't mean it towards them but that is how they took it." Yes they didn't have to react to it like that. They could have called you and sent a message privately, but you have the power to change that entire situation. You can throw flames in the fire or you can try to step into their shoes, and see their point of view and apologize that they felt it was about them. My friend said, "It was a blanket statement for all married people." Some people on Facebook take your posts personally and others do not. You can post whatever you want on Facebook but be mindful of what you post. Be the better person and apologize to those who take offense to it. My friend was right. That night I meditated on his words and immediately I really got it. I knew in my heart I meant no harm to them. Because I did love them, it was easy for me to swallow my pride even though I didn't agree with how they handled it. That situation changed my relationship with some of them but it really changed me. I realize that when I swallow my pride, I allow spirit to take over. When spirit takes over everyone learns a lesson and it leaves no bitterness. There will be times when your pride gets bruised or someone takes something the wrong way as in the situation above.

Don't get upset just stop and think. I could be wrong and no matter if I feel I was right, I still hurt someone's feelings. Being right is not important. Ezra Benson said," pride is concerned with being right and humility is concerned with what is right." Showing humility is putting the feelings of others before your own and it takes a strong person to do that. Whoever said that people who are humble are weak is crazy. Now it has been more difficult for me to show humility to people I don't know, but I am getting better at that too. I am learning to not process everything thrown at me. There are times when people I don't really know blurted insults to me or were just rude to me. I just say to myself, "wow they are really miserable" and I say a prayer for them. Smiling and just walking away is a gift. Now I am not always successful but I am still a work in progress. I can tell you this, the more you practice humility the better you do get at it. I challenge you to apply humility to a situation you may have. If you feel you were right in a situation, or there was some type of incident that you said some angry things to someone. Lower your pride, apologize, and let spirit take over. I read that humility is the mother of all virtues and it really is. There is a quote by Dwight Moody that says, "God sends no one away empty except those who are full of themselves." Don't let your pride ruin your relationships with others. Be mindful of the type of energy you are emitting out into the Universe. Substitute pride with humility and the Universe will bow to you. Remember you have purpose to be here and you can't afford to get off the road of your destiny. Pride can quickly knock you off the road but humility will bring you closer to your destiny.

CHAPTER 15
FINDING LOVE

Love isn't something you find. Love finds you.

– Anonymous

I can honestly say that I have been blessed when it comes to love because I have learned everything not to do. Now that I am 40 years old I finally get it. It frustrates me that all these years have passed me and I had it wrong. Until you truly love yourself and you are happy with yourself will love find you. Yes love will find you. You don't go looking for love. You are love and because you are love you don't need to find it. It goes back to attraction. When your light shines you will attract people to you.

It wasn't until I learned to love myself and get in touch with my spirit is when men would approach me. Especially if I have a conversation with a man, they would always say, "I really enjoyed our talk." Then I will get this line, "There is something about you!" Most men do use that line but you can feel when it's genuine and when it is not. As a woman and most single women, we don't feel complete without a man. That is the wrong expectation to have. We need to stop looking for someone to complete us because we should be complete by ourselves. A spouse is supposed to add to you, not complete you. I did believe that illusion that there are no good men out there. The truth is that I was not on a level of awareness where I could see good men because I always hated the men in my past and would never let it go. Basically, it is really simple but there is some work you have to do. In order to find love we have to find it in ourselves and stop looking for it. When you are single, your focus should be always on how to better yourself and be a better you. Learn to enjoy yourself. Take yourself to the movies or to dinner. Take that time to get to know you and to just love on you. You will shine brighter than any jewel and become that woman a man has been praying for. Let go of those past hurts from relationships that didn't work. You have to stop dwelling in the past. Get into the present moment of now. Remember your soul is not the past, it's not in the future but it is in the now waiting on you to catch up. Your soul can't guide you when you are stuck on what happened in the past. If you are dating someone just be you. Don't put on an act to try to be something you are not. If you are funny and like to tell jokes, be that. Be honest about your feelings, what you want and don't want. If you want to be married and he does not, stop seeing him. Again, focus on loving you and enjoy loving you. That will attract love to you.

CHAPTER 16
ACTIVISM

Activism is simply having the courage to
stand up to fear.

- Oyin

Being an Activist in North Tulsa has to be
one of the most challenging things I have
ever done in my life. Activism is not for
the faint at heart. Each fight for justice
truly is like a boxing match because just
like a boxer in a ring; you will take many
punches. You're left with scars and you
better get up before the referee counts to
ten. Tulsa is truly a city divided and is one
of the most racist cities on this planet. In
2012, city councilor Jack Henderson
proposed to turn the name of the street
Cincinnati into Martin Luther King Blvd.
The street name was changed but since
Cincinnati now known as Martin Luther
King Blvd ran right through downtown;
white business owners were furious about

the name change. They did not want a street named Martin Luther King Blvd to run through their places of businesses and homes. To no surprise of course they made a big fuss about it so Martin Luther King Blvd stops at Archer St downtown and on the other side of the street; the street sign stays Cincinnati. Tulsa is the home of Black Wall Street and the prosperous town of Greenwood. Greenwood was home to black millionaires who owned planes. Yes black millionaires who owned planes! Greenwood had everything and many black entertainers would come to Greenwood. Today, if you ask most black people who live here about Greenwood, they really can't tell you much. All they will tell you is that there was a riot here in 1921. My cousin Chief doesn't like to refer to what happened in 1921 as a riot, but as a massacre. A riot implies that two parties violently disturbed peace, but in truth what happened to the residents of

Greenwood was nothing but a massacre. The massacre that happened in 1921 has silenced so many people even into the next generation. Black folks today will walk or drive right past Greenwood and are totally not affected by it. The Brady District is a booming area in downtown Tulsa. It is named after Tate Brady who played a role in The Massacre of 1921. You can see his name on buildings and signs all over downtown: The Cain's Ballroom (which used to be Tate Brady's garage), Brady Heights, Brady Theater, Brady Street, and The Brady District. In 2013, Chief and I met with Lee Roy Chapman at This Land Press which is a media company in Tulsa that prints newspapers. Lee Roy Chapman was a historian who loved history. However, he wasn't what you would picture as a historian with his many tattoos and long beard. Through Lee Roy's research he discovered that Tate Brady was a member of The Ku Klux Klan and had a role in the

Massacre of 1921. He had tried to let others know and even taken this information to others but always failed at getting someone to really take interest in it. Well through our discovery, Chief and I decided that everyone needs to know about this and that we have to take Tate Brady's name off the street. We felt that no survivor of 1921 should have to see that man's name everyday of their life. So we challenged City Council to rename the street. It was a long and hard fight and the racial tensions were on high. The story went national. I couldn't believe the hateful things that were said about us and just the racist comments in general. I knew that racism existed but I had never experienced it this way. I would read national articles and their comments, and then I would read the articles and comments here in Tulsa. The comments from white people outside of Oklahoma were in support of the change but the comments from majority of white people in Oklahoma were against the change. The City Councilors were getting emails and calls from their constituents demanding that they do not change the name of the street or they wouldn't vote for them again. At the last City Council meeting there was a 7-1 vote to change the street from Brady St to M.B. Brady St. City Councilor Jeanie Cue cried tears as she told us that she couldn't go against her constituents. I couldn't believe what I was witnessing. A white woman is crying right in my face telling me how sorry she is because she had to side with her racist constituents. Thinking about this now chokes me up. It chokes me up not because I sympathized with Jeanie Cue, but that Jeanie Cue didn't have the courage to stand up for what is right in the face of racism. That entire experience taught me that racism is alive and well. If we are to ever do anything about racism we have to expose it, not ignore it. Chief and I had a conversation after the city council meeting and I said, "Well we lost!" Chief said, "No we didn't!" We started a dialogue that would have never taken place. As time went by, The Brady District just kept growing and growing. They even started to have Juneteenth celebrations in The Brady District to attract black folks to come and spend their money there. We have always had Juneteenth on Greenwood but the past few years they had not been as successful as they have been in the past. All kinds of entertainers would come and perform and thousands of people of all races would sit on their blankets and enjoy the food and music. It was beautiful. Now for the past two years, black musicians and majority of black folks attend Juneteenth celebrations in The Brady District. We have two Juneteenth Celebrations. One on Greenwood and one in The Brady District at a park called, The Guthrie Green. The excuses I get from Black folk is that the entertainment is better. The excuses I get from Black musicians is that they get paid in The Brady District and on Greenwood they do not. Again, I couldn't believe what I was witnessing. It truly breaks my heart to see black folks so easily led by entertainment and money, and totally forget about rebuilding what we have right here on Black Wall Street. I look at other communities of people from Chinatown, Hispanic communities, and Jewish communities that thrive. They all support their own in their own communities. Chief would say that you would never see Jewish people have a party in Auschwitz. Jewish people have the motto, "Never forget!" It always troubles me that we as a people do not have that type of unity. It is one of our biggest downfalls. Until black folks in Tulsa understand this, Greenwood and Black Wall Street will no longer exist. The Brady District has always had plans to take Greenwood and they are already sitting within two blocks of Greenwood today. While we are there partying and spending our dollars there, they are steadily eating up Greenwood bit by bit. It's self-hate within ourselves and we don't even realize the damage we cause by not being organized and unified. If our Ancestors from Greenwood came back to North Tulsa today they would be appalled to see what it has become. Our black leaders in North Tulsa are all intelligent individuals but many lack the backbone to stand up against racism. They all try to work around it and most just have given up on dealing with it and start to focus on themselves. North Tulsa has lost the true meaning of community, and lacks that drive that was once here at the beginning of Greenwood. I don't know what it is about the mindset of most black folks today, but we are so afraid of building our own. We get all caught up in the kumbaya moments of equality. When you go and visit Asian businesses and Hispanic businesses within their communities you see no one else working in their businesses but them. We as a people will not even support our own. We as African Americans have the highest buying power; In 2015 Black Enterprise announced that we rank $1.1 trillion in buying power. We just made other people rich and yet we still struggle. The question lingers in my mind, "How do we change that?" Being an Activist it hurts to see that your own people will not wake up. More and more black folks are waking up now but it's not enough and we are sure not waking up fast enough. What this experience has really taught me is that I need to understand the power of collective economics and understand the power of building community. Many of us do not celebrate Kwanzaa. I really started getting into it last year. Kwanzaa teaches those core principles such as: unity, self-determination, faith, creativity, purpose, collective economics and collective work, and responsibility. Imagine if our parents celebrated Kwanzaa and instilled those principles in us from an early age instead of us believing that a fat white man in a red suit would bring us gifts. We would be ahead of the game in this society. It has been important for me to teach my children these qualities and share them with others.

DISCLAIMER

The information in this book is based from my own life experiences. In no way am I a counselor or claim to have all the answers about life. Believe me when I say that I am not perfect and I make mistakes in my life. I am not the same person I was yesterday and I am forever changing. It is not my intent to defame or humiliate anyone in this book.

REFERENCES

Information from Deepak, Dr. Wayne Dyer, and Eckhart Tolle were researched from lectures on YouTube and quotes collected from their Facebook pages. Black Enterprise Magazine and Huffington Post were sources of information.